ideals
CHRISTMAS

May the peace and love of Jesus Christ
Go with you on your way,
And bless your home and loved ones
In spirit Christmas Day.

May the joy of God's bright promise—
The Advent of His Son—
Live evermore within each heart
And comfort everyone.

May the faith of old-time prophets
Be with you where you are,
And may the truth of God's own Word
Remain your Christmas Star.

Helen Shick

Publisher, James A. Kuse
Managing Editor, Ralph Luedtke
Editor/Ideals, Colleen Callahan Gonring
Associate Editor, Linda Robinson
Production Manager, Mark Brunner
Photographic Editor, Gerald Koser
Copy Editor, Norma Barnes
Art Editor, Duane Weaver
Contributing Editor, Beverly Wiersum Charette

ISBN 0-89542-336-7 295

IDEALS—Vol. 37, No. 8 November MCMLXXX. IDEALS (ISSN 0019-137X) is published eight times a year,
January, February, April, June, July, September, October, November
by IDEALS PUBLISHING CORPORATION, 11315 Watertown Plank Road, Milwaukee, Wis. 53226
Second class postage paid at Milwaukee, Wisconsin. Copyright © MCMLXXX by IDEALS PUBLISHING CORPORATION.
All rights reserved. Title IDEALS registered U.S. Patent Office.
Published Simultaneously in Canada.

ONE YEAR SUBSCRIPTION—eight consecutive issues as published—$15.95
TWO YEAR SUBSCRIPTION—sixteen consecutive issues as published—$27.95
SINGLE ISSUES—$2.95

The cover and entire contents of IDEALS are fully protected by copyright and must
not be reproduced in any manner whatsoever. Printed and bound in U.S.A.

Long-Ago Christmas

Long ago, at Christmastime,
How thrilled we all would be
When our dad would say to us,
"Let's go and find our tree."

What fun we'd have looking
For a very special kind;
It must be the finest tree
That we could possibly find.

They were all so lovely,
Throughout the woodland scene,
But at last we'd come upon
A very beautiful evergreen.

We'd start for home, so gaily,
Carrying our chosen tree.
We could hardly wait until
Our mom, back home, could see.

The lovely tree went on a stand,
After we were tucked in bed,
And all the dreams of Christmas
Would fill each sleepy head.

Ah, then, on Christmas morning,
What a glorious, lovely sight!
It seemed a group of fairies
Had worked there through the night.

For all the lovely branches,
Were full of so many things:
Glowing candles and tinsel gay,
Popcorn and peppermint canes.

We still have a Christmas
That is beautiful in every way,
But memories of those long ago,
Are in our hearts to stay.

Doris Connell

MERRY CHRISTMAS

At Christmastime Mom kept our kitchen a buzzin'
By baking us cookies dozen after dozen.

She gathered huge bowls and long, wooden spoons,
And gave our house warmth those cold afternoons.

Sugar was scooped from a canister of tin,
And flour was sifted from out of its bin.

The fragrance of vanilla and eggs filled the air,
Then slowly the buttermilk was added with care.

I watched every movement she made, quite in awe
Of the mixing and stirring and blending I saw.

A great mound of dough, floured and fat,
Was kneaded and rolled until it was flat.

The cutters were carefully chosen by me:
Santa, an angel, candy cane, Christmas tree.

Then onto a cookie sheet we placed each one,
And baked them eight minutes until they were done.

We swirled on the icing, choosing between
Three different colors: red, white or green.

A dash of bright speckles was added on top,
Then we tasted a sample before we would stop.

Now each year at Christmas when I make this dough
My kitchen holds memories of that one long ago.

While the cookies are baking and stacking up high,
The joy of past Christmases lingers close by.

Deborah George Hyland

Moravian Christmas Cookies

Dorothy Gladys Spicer

In the Pennsylvania Dutch country Moravian Christmas cookies—both white and brown—are made from heirloom cutters of engaging design. The cutters, which in many families have come down for several generations, include such familiar shapes as rabbits, cocks, horses, and birds, as well as stars and hearts. Some claim the idea of baking animal cookies stems from ancient times, when living creatures were sacrificed to Teutonic deities at the Feast of the Winter Solstice. Many believed that cakes in animal form gradually took the place of the original offerings. Centuries later, the Christ Child's Feast supplanted earlier pagan ceremonies, and Christian usage retained animal cakes along with other heathen symbols, such as mistletoe, lights, and jovial revels.

Christmas Eve was a holy night to the early Pennsylvania Dutch. On the anniversary of His birth, *Grishtkindel*, the Christ Child, reputedly rode a lowly ass from farm to farm with gifts and cookies for little ones. The farmer always remembered Grishtkindel's beast with a pile of hay in the barnyard. Next morning, he portioned out the fodder—now soaked with "Christmas dew"—to cows, horses, and other farm animals. For this food, blessed by the Christ Child's presence, supposedly made creatures fecund and healthy throughout the year.

The farmer's wife, also, believed in the Christmas dew. What was beneficial to animals surely was good for human beings! So she placed bread outside the window at night. Before breakfast on Christmas Day, the family gathered around her. To each person—from the baby to grandparents—she gave a piece of the consecrated loaf and expressed a wish for happiness and good health.

The Pennsylvania Dutch people brought over from the Rhineland many other Christmas customs which, when transplanted to new soil, gradually assumed a distinctive New World flavor. There was *Belsnickel*, for example, who visited children long before they had even heard of Santa Claus. There was little of the benign old Saint about Belsnickel.

The role of this disagreeable character usually was assumed by some local youth who disguised his identity with a mask, beard, and furry garments. He carried a long curling whip, or a bundle of switches. He made rounds by candlelight and announced his arrival by loud scratchings on the windowpane. When Belsnickel was admitted to the kitchen, little ones huddled close to their elders. For he had a mean habit of inquiring into past behavior and then tossing nuts and candies to the floor. Whenever children stooped to snatch a sweet, Belsnickel's whip either shot out and coiled about their feet, or else smacked smartly from behind. After a few such warnings the young could retrieve the goodies.

Belsnickel no longer menaces the Pennsylvania Dutch country, where today some of the most tender and beautiful of all Christmas traditions are observed.

The Moravian settlement of Bethlehem—named after the town where Jesus was born—celebrates the Holy Birth with a candlelight service. During the final hymn young men and women bring in trays with lighted beeswax candles, locally made. Each worshiper takes a candle—a symbol of the Light of the World.

The service concludes with the ancient Love Feast consisting of Moravian buns and coffee—for on this night all are brothers. As the ceremonies end, children rush home to presents, lighted trees, and the *putz*, or nativity scene, with its ingenious small figures. The putzes, which are typical of native folk art tradition, play an important part in all Christmas festivities. *Putzing*, or visiting from door to door to see neighborhood nativities, is an old custom at Bethlehem. Formerly householders invited in all visitors—whether strangers or friends—for wine and Moravian Christmas cookies; but nowadays—with a larger community and more strangers about—only friends and acquaintances receive hospitality.

Today Pennsylvania Dutch Christmas trees, like their hospitality, have undergone subtle changes. Electric bulbs, commercial ornaments, and balls of colored glass now largely replace the lighted candles, polished apples, and animal cookies that once made every tree a triumph of family craftmanship. Although cookies no longer hang from the fragrant boughs as often as formerly, both children and adults devour the little cakes with as much gusto as ever.

Recipes for white and dark Moravian Christmas cookies follow. Both are delicious. The white are more delicate, the brown spicy and exciting. Cut the thinly rolled dough into animal shapes, sprinkle freely with colored sugars, and serve to holiday visitors with coffee, tea, or wine.

For Holiday Giving . . .

Gifts from the Kitchen

Gingerbread Cookies

2 c. flour
1 t. baking powder
¼ t. baking soda
1 t. cinnamon
½ t. ginger
⅓ c. sugar
½ c. shortening
½ c. molasses
3 T. hot water

Combine all ingredients in a large bowl. Blend well. Chill dough at least 1 hour before handling. Roll out dough on floured surface to ⅛-inch thickness. Cut with gingerbread man cookie cutter. Place on ungreased cookie sheets. Bake at 400° for 8 to 10 minutes. Cool and decorate.

Moravian White Christmas Cookies

2 c. butter
3 c. sugar
5 eggs
1 t. baking soda, dissolved in 4 T. boiling water
4 to 5 c. sifted all-purpose flour
1 c. cream

Thoroughly cream butter and sugar, beating until very light. Beat eggs well and add, blending well. Stir in soda mixture. Sift flour and add gradually, alternating with cream. Mix thoroughly. The dough should be stiff. Form into ball, wrap in waxed paper, and chill in refrigerator for several hours. Roll dough out thinly on floured board and cut into fancy shapes. Decorate with colored sugars, nuts, or candied fruits, if desired. Bake in a 350° oven about 12 minutes.

Moravian Dark Christmas Cookies

3¾ c. flour
¾ t. baking soda
¾ t. ginger
¾ t. cloves
¾ t. cinnamon
½ t. allspice
½ t. nutmeg
   Dash of salt
1 c. molasses
½ c. butter
⅓ c. brown sugar, firmly packed

Sift together the flour, spices, salt, and soda. Heat molasses and butter until butter melts, add sugar, and stir until dissolved. Gradually add flour, beating after each addition until dough is smooth. Cover with waxed paper and store in refrigerator about a week. Then roll out dough thinly, a small amount at a time. Cut into fancy shapes and decorate, as desired. Bake in a 350° oven for 6 minutes, or until done.

Springerle

4 eggs
2 c. sugar
4½ c. flour
   Anise seed

Beat eggs until light and creamy. Add sugar gradually, beating until dissolved. Stir in flour until well blended. Chill several hours or overnight. Roll out ⅛ inch thick. If desired, press a floured springerle rolling pin on dough to emboss designs. Cut into squares. Transfer cookies onto a board that has been sprinkled with anise seed and additional flour. Let dry for 12 hours. Place cookies on greased baking sheet. Bake at 325° for 12 to 15 minutes. Makes about 9 dozen cookies.

365 Days of Christmas

ENJOY CHRISTmas!
It's His birthday.
ENJOY LIFE!
It's His way!

If visions of sugar plums dance in your head and Christmas is still months away, what should you do? If thoughts of Kris Kringle, reindeer and elves, dazzling Christmas trees and the sound of Christmas carols persist in July, where can you go? Do what two million other people do every year: Visit the fabulous one-acre salesroom of Bronner's Christmas Decorations in the picturesque German town of Frankenmuth in mid-Michigan—open 361 days of the year.

Bronner's defies description. Journalists have dipped into their vocabularies and come up with phrases such as "Disneyland of the Christmas World," "Christmas Fantasy Land," "Christmas Ornament Capital of the World," "Bronner's Fairyland," and "Christmas Spectacular." Others have said visiting the place is like taking a trip to the North Pole, that it is the Santa Claus Land of their early childhood or a transplanted scene from a Grimm's fairy tale. It is all of these and more.

The architecture of Bronner's store, located at 25 Christmas Lane, is Bavarian and Alpine, with bell cots and a red crushed tile roof. The inside of the structure was designed to give the impression of an Alpine village, its cluster of small shops readied for the Yuletide.

The visitor leaves the work-a-day world behind as he approaches the building, for a complete life-size Nativity scene in a foliage-and-rock setting reminds him of the real meaning of Christmas.

One is bedazzled upon entering the great showroom, for all around him is animation, and a million ever-moving lights dance on the ceiling and displays, reflected from the slowly turning, suspended, over-sized, multi-mirrored balls. A prominently placed clock dial gives one the time: half-past March, a quarter to September, or straight-up December. Subdued, piped-in Christmas carols fill the area and surround the visitor, setting just the right atmosphere for browsing and selecting new tree ornaments to go with the old. It is estimated that a leisurely "walk-through" takes about two hours. There is no feeling of being crowded because the emporium was designed to accommodate as many as 1500 people at one time. On an average weekend day, about 15,000 people enter Bronner's door. It should be noted here that the parking lot will accommodate 250 cars and 24 buses.

Unlike most displays of merchandise that appear static, in Bronner's, animated figures greet one at every turn: choirboys, carolers, Santa Claus and Mrs. Santa Claus, reindeer, elves—warming themselves over a fire or making toys in Santa's workshop—beavers gnawing on sticks of wood with snowbirds watching, and many, many "people" and "animals" swinging, rocking, trimming trees or what have you. The place is alive—with action, color, lights.

A fifteen-foot snowman welcomes the visitor to the area devoted to what Mr. Bronner calls a "live catalog" of decorations for use by municipalities, churches, stores, malls, and corporations. Two-thirds of the business is tied to about one thousand commercial accounts, with individual sales making up the remainder. Many mail-order houses get much of their merchandise here.

The large, fully carpeted showroom is organized into areas or "shops": Christmas jewelry, ornaments, wreaths and garlands, Hummel figures, German Christmas music books, candles, etc. The store is known particularly for its Christmas tree ornaments: over three thousand styles of artistic mouth-blown glass ornaments, some carrying greetings in almost every language.

In a special museum room, away from the main exhibit area and open exclusively to groups at specific times, is a distinguished feature collection, including a large teardrop shaped ornament bearing a religious painting done by an Italian artist. The museum also boasts an extensive display of Hummel figures in a setting showing steps in the production of these popular, much-loved figurines. In the Hummel corner of the salesroom, visitors

can then purchase the figurines, from the moderately priced familiar small-size figurine to a large one which carries a price tag of $12,500.

The Tannenbaum Shop displays many different kinds of Christmas trees, tastefully trimmed and lighted by the store's specialist in tree decoration. Each carries a special theme and color scheme. Decorations for the trees come from twenty-five countries. One might see Baby's First Tree—a tiny white one with pastel satin ornaments—as well as large ones featuring decorations such as snowflakes, ornaments related to the Nativity, to toyland or to Christmas in other lands. (The tree-trimming expert suggests that the most meaningful ornaments be placed at eye-level for greatest enjoyment.)

Decorative nutcrackers (in the shape of little men, of course), reminiscent of the famous story told in ballet to the music of Tchaikovsky's *Nutcracker Suite*, music boxes, and numerous other

"gifts for all seasons and reasons" greet the eye.

Bronner's has no less than five hundred different kinds and sizes of Nativity scenes with figures running from one inch in height to life-size. Some are made of straw, some of olive wood, some of ceramics. The largest Nativity scene exhibited is a seventeen-piece commercial grouping that may be had for $6,000.

Of course there are closets full of Santa Claus suits. One famous customer was John Wayne, who, on December 15, 1977, ordered a Santa Claus suit "with a natural appearing wig and beard."

Who are the people responsible for this mammoth business? What are they like? Wallace Bronner, who, the year round, wears a poinsettia-red jacket with holly in his lapel, and his wife, Irene, started the business in a very humble way. Mr. Bronner began as a painter of cardboard and wooden signs for window displays, car sales, etc., in a room over his aunt's grocery store. An order for a Christmas display in a hardware store in a nearby city opened the door. Soon he was asked to create decorations for light poles and shopping centers, along with Nativity scenes for churches. A retail business was established, with Wallace and Irene in full partnership, that outgrew three buildings in downtown Frankenmuth. The two-million dollar project in which the Bronners now do business was opened to the public in June, 1977.

Governor William Milliken has designated Bronner's Christmas Decorations as an Embassy of Michigan Tourism. The citation reads: "I bestow this honor and its attendant privileges and responsibilities in recognition of outstanding and significant contributions to the Michigan Tourist Industry."

Like the great majority of people in Frankenmuth, who are descendants of German missionaries who came to this country in 1845 to minister to the Indians, both Wallace and Irene are devoted Christians, active in church and community affairs. Mr. Bronner says, "The Christmas season is an especially joyful time of the year. I truly believe that the real glow should come from the warmth in people's hearts. Our job here is to provide gifts and decorations for a birthday party—the birthday of Christ. Our business was built on the idea of celebrating the Christ Child's birthday every day of our lives—not just limiting our celebration to the traditional twelve days of Christmas." The Bronners' motto therefore is: "365 Days of Christmas."

Doris A. Paul

A Winter Day

'Tis Christmas again and once more as before
We hang up the holly outside the front door.
The hills and valleys are covered with snow,
Brushed with crystals of ice that glow.
From towering trees, from shrubs, each tiny strand
Glistens in winter's fairyland.
The snow, like a veil, drawn across earth's face,
Falls from each branch like frothy lace
And the wind fingers lightly hill and plain,
Chanting a soft cathedral strain;
Through the windowed trees, the sun's clear, bright gaze
Cloaks the world in a golden haze,
Transforming this earthly vision of ice
To reflection of Paradise.
'Tis Christmas again and once more as before
We hang up the holly outside the front door.

Margaret Phillips Succop

Christmas

My sisters and I began preparations for Christmas well ahead. . . . I do not pretend to remember the gifts that we found on Christmas morning. I know that we hung our long stockings from the mantel behind the tall base burner in the living room. I know that for many years each of us was certain to find a shiny dime, an orange, and a bag of candy when we came downstairs. What I remember is something deeper and something richer. One of the memories is the afternoon of the day before Christmas, when Father and I took a hand ax and together climbed the orchard slope and went into the evergreen grove beyond the apple trees.

For years getting the Christmas tree was an annual ritual. It was a leisurely expedition, and we took our time in walking the woodland and searching for just the right tree. Father wanted a tree about seven feet high—a spruce with evenly balanced limbs and a strong top spike.

The evergreen woodland in December was a peaceful sanctuary. Some years the snow had come and the Temple Mountains across the Contoocook Valley were sparkling in the slanting rays.

Sometimes it was a gray, quiet day with the countryside brooding in the hushed waiting period before the snow.

I remember how we trimmed the Christmas tree after supper on Christmas Eve. Probably it would be more accurate to say that Mother and sisters trimmed the tree. I can still see those shoe boxes of ornaments. All year long they sat on the top shelf of the front hall closet. There were long strands of silvery tinsel, fragile, red balls, and red paper bells that folded like accordions. During the day, my sisters made long strings of red cranberries and strands of white popcorn. I can see the brown gingerbread men that Mother made—always four of them so each of us could have one. Then Father stood on a chair and fastened the big, gleaming, white star to the top spike. When all the trimmings were on, we brought our presents from their hiding places. The bigger parcels went on the floor beneath the branches, smaller packages were placed among the upper branches.

When the tree was trimmed and all the presents ready for Christmas morning, Father took his well-worn Bible, and while we listened, he read again the old, but ever-new and thrilling story of the Wise Men who followed a guiding star and came to the Babe in the Manger. That, I think, is what I remember best over the years. It would not have been Christmas without the story. And when a lad took his lamp and climbed the steep stairs to his room, he remembered Father's words. "Someday, somehow, men will learn to live in peace and goodwill." The years are many and the years are long. But a grown man remembers those words. Someday, somehow, all men will be brothers. That must be our hope, for there is no other way.

Haydn S. Pearson

Selection is reprinted from *The New England Year* by Haydn S. Pearson, with the permission of W.W. Norton & Company, Inc. Copyright © 1966 by W. W. Norton & Company, Inc.

The Sounds of Christmas

The sounds of Christmas fill the air
  This special time of year,
The sound of little ones at play,
  Their laughter loud and clear,
A little girl, a little boy,
  With bright and shining eyes,
The glow of gladness in their hearts,
  The look of sweet surprise.

The sounds of Christmas fill each home
  From dawn unto the night,
As children check their Christmas lists
  In childish, sweet delight.
The little ones do romp about,
  Each little girl and boy,
A precious part of Christmastime
  To treasure and enjoy.

The sounds of Christmas hold a charm
  That everyone might store,
And in each greeting, you will find
  A special Christmas prayer,
For peace and hope, for faith and love,
  The joy of childish laughter,
A Merry Christmas day, and then
  A happy "all year after".

Garnett Ann Schultz

The Coming
of Santa Claus

Old, jolly, merry Santa Claus
Again is on his way.
I almost now can see the toys
Upon his loaded sleigh.

I seem to hear the reindeer prance,
And on the breeze, there swells
A sound that could not sweeter be,
The music of the bells.

This mystery, profound and strange,
Pervading all the air,
May be explained in just this way,
That Santa's everywhere.

Clear out the fireplace to make room
For him to jump inside,
That he may fill the stockings full,
That hang along its side.

And plant your Christmas trees about,
All decked with colors gay,
That strangers may the spirit feel,
Who pass along the way.

Then be a Santa Claus yourself,
And you will quickly see
It does not need great wealth or gold,
A Santa Claus to be.

Agnes Davenport Bond

Billie the Brownie

Raymond McBride

Shortly before Thanksgiving in 1930, "Billie the Brownie" aired for the first time on WTMJ-Radio in Milwaukee, Wisconsin, as a five-minute promotion. Its primary purpose was to attract listeners to the annual Christmas parade sponsored by Schusters, a Milwaukee department store. The radio show, however, accomplished a great deal more; when the five minutes were up, the sponsor had a hit.

For the next quarter of a century, generations of children were glued to their radios from 5:00 to 5:15 P.M., Monday through Friday during the weeks before Christmas. Besides hearing Uncle Larry and Billie the Brownie read letters from children to Santa Claus and stories from the "Magic Book," little listeners were treated to Santa's "Ho, ho, ho," from the North Pole, assuring them that all their letters had been received, read, and, no doubt, would be answered. After twenty-five years, some of these listeners were children of the children who had listened to the early shows.

What was the big attraction? The letters to Santa. As soon as the program first aired, they started pouring in.

Although Uncle Larry and Billie could read only a few a day, children listened at home breathlessly to learn if theirs were among the lucky few. The first year the program drew about thirty-five thousand letters, every one answered by Santa and his helpers at the store. By the end of the show's long run in 1955, Santa had received 1,500,000 pieces of mail.

The show's great success can be attributed in part to its creator, Larry Teich—Uncle Larry. A pioneer broadcaster, Teich covered everything, including the first football game ever broadcast from Camp Randall Stadium at the University of Wisconsin in Madison. He was WTMJ's first announcer and the producer of such children's shows as "Seckatary Hawkins" and Captain Larry's "Our Club."

For "Billie the Brownie," Teich came up with all kinds of stories. One of them, "The Star and the Christmas Tree," was recorded by RCA Victor and distributed nationally. Uncle Larry and Billie read the stories when the "Magic Book" was opened by the children listening at home, who chorused, "I've been good, I've been good."

An experienced director, Teich selected local actors and actresses to play the parts in "Billie the Brownie." Over the years there were half a dozen Billie the Brownies—all women—several Santa Clauses and Mrs. Clauses, and other characters, such as the barking dog, Willie Wagtail, and Me-Tik, Santa's Eskimo driver, who never said anything.

These characters became as real and beloved as Santa himself. I remember that when our eldest son, now thirty-two, got his first dog, he naturally insisted upon naming it Willie Wagtail. At Christmastime there was always a run on bones at butcher shops by children who wanted to leave them out for Willie along with a cup of coffee for Santa and sugar for his reindeer.

One Billie the Brownie, for four years running, was Carol Cotter, who now makes documentaries for station WHA-TV in Madison. Her son, Dave Begel, recalls that he and his younger brother used to listen to the program, never realizing that Billie was their mother.

"She would leave for work at four o'clock. My brother and I listened to the show every day, and one thing we never figured out was why our letters got read on the air every year. It made quite an impression on the kids in the neighborhood."

The reason that Begel and his brother did not recognize their mother's voice is that it was high-pitched. "Peter Pannish" is the way Begel describes it. Later, when Begel was old enough and the secret was out, his mother taught him the Billie the Brownie voice.

"Even today," says Begel, now thirty-six, "I get a thrill when I go to parties around Christmas and people talk about the old 'Billie the Brownie' shows."

Other people now in their twenties and thirties also recall the magic of the show:

"I thought there were real people in that little box," said one man.

"When I was a girl, Billie the Brownie was as important to me as Santa Claus himself," a woman said. "I pictured Billie as six inches tall."

When discussions were held on whether to transfer the show to television, Larry Teich rebelled, arguing that brownies were invisible.

What he was talking about is the one big advantage radio still has over television—illusion. Teich knew that children would not believe in brownies that they could see. They might even have questioned whether Santa was really Santa Claus. So, inevitably, "Billie the Brownie" ended, a victim of the excitement of television's advent.

No matter what they do or do not remember about the show, no one can forget the big moment, which came, of course, on Christmas Eve. On earlier shows, Santa had created suspense with technicalities that threatened to delay his departure from the North Pole, while children at home groaned anxiously. Eventually though, Mrs. Claus admonished her husband with, "Hurry, Santa! If you don't get going, you won't get around the world tonight!" Then Santa climbed into his sleigh, "to his team gave a whistle," and off the reindeer went, with all the appropriate sound effects: runners creaking through the snow, the snap of the whip and, finally, the sound of sleigh bells fading in the distance. Santa's departure was always followed by a reading of "The Night Before Christmas."

When Gimbels bought Schusters, "Billie the Brownie" came with the deal. But in the 1950s something emerged to replace much of radio entertainment—television.

Larry Teich went on to become, at various times, a labor official and lobbyist, an official for the Office of Price Stabilization and an official for the American Automobile Association. He retired in 1968 and died in 1978, at seventy-five. Only then did many people find out who had created one of their favorite radio shows, "Billie the Brownie."

Larry Teich was a friend of mine. Away from radio, Larry was not an overly talkative man, almost dour. Only occasionally did he show a rather dry, droll sense of humor. I cannot remember him or anyone else ever mentioning "Billie the Brownie" whenever we got together.

But there is no doubt that in "Billie the Brownie" Larry had a hit show. Many people have told me they wish "Billie" would return to the air, for their children. Maybe it is an idea whose time has gone, but has come back again.

A Visit from St. Nicholas

Clement C. Moore

'Twas the night before Christmas, when all through the house
Not a creature was stirring, not even a mouse;
The stockings were hung by the chimney with care
In hopes that St. Nicholas soon would be there;
The children were nestled all snug in their beds,
While visions of sugarplums danced through their heads;
And Mamma in her 'kerchief, and I in my cap,
Had just settled our brains for a long winter's nap—
When out on the lawn there arose such a clatter,
I sprang from my bed to see what was the matter;
Away to the window I flew like a flash,
Tore open the shutters and threw up the sash.
The moon on the breast of the new-fallen snow
Gave the luster of midday to objects below;
When, what to my wondering eyes should appear,
But a miniature sleigh, and eight tiny reindeer,
With a little old driver, so lively and quick,
I knew in a moment it must be St. Nick.
More rapid than eagles his coursers they came,
And he whistled, and shouted, and called them by name:
"Now, Dasher! Now, Dancer! Now, Prancer and Vixen!
On, Comet! On Cupid! On, Donner and Blitzen!
To the top of the porch! To the top of the wall!
Now, dash away! Dash away! Dash away all!"
As dry leaves that before the wild hurricane fly,
When they meet with an obstacle, mount to the sky,
So up to the housetop the coursers they flew,
With a sleigh full of toys—and St. Nicholas, too!
And then, in a twinkling, I heard on the roof,
The prancing and pawing of each little hoof.
As I drew in my head, and was turning around,
Down the chimney St. Nicholas came with a bound.
He was dressed all in fur, from his head to his foot,
And his clothes were all tarnished with ashes and soot!
A bundle of toys he had flung on his back,
And he looked like a peddler just opening his pack;
His eyes—how they twinkled! His dimples, how merry!
His cheeks were like roses, his nose like a cherry!
His droll little mouth was drawn up like a bow,
And the beard of his chin was as white as the snow,
The stump of a pipe he held tight in his teeth,
And the smoke, it encircled his head like a wreath.
He had a broad face, and a little round belly,
That shook, when he laugh'd, like a bowlful of jelly.
He was chubby and plump, a right jolly old elf;
And I laughed, when I saw him, in spite of myself.

A wink of his eye, and a twist of his head,
Soon gave me to know I had nothing to dread.
He spoke not a word, but went straight to his work,
And filled all the stockings—then turned with a jerk,
And laying his fingers aside of his nose,
And giving a nod, up the chimney he rose.
He sprang to his sleigh, to his team gave a whistle,
And away they all flew, like the down off a thistle.
But I heard him exclaim, ere he drove out of sight,
"Happy Christmas to all! And to all a good night!"

A Christmas Song

Joyfully upon the air
There comes a sweet refrain,
For carols bring the message
That it's Christmastime again.

Music ringing round the town
Proclaims the Savior's birth,
Filling hearts with hope anew
Of peace to men on earth.

Harken to the angels' song;
Let earth receive her King;
Filled with spirit, loud and strong,
Lift up your voice and sing.

Keep in your heart a Christmas song,
And let the words convey
The message of the carols
To all men this Christmas day.

Mildred L. Jarrell

Christmas Happiness

Christmas is happiness found everywhere,
In the song of "White Christmas" that floats through the air;
In the sweet, ancient carols that glowingly sing
Of the Child born in Bethlehem—the King over Kings.
Christmas is hustle and bustle in stores;
It is red ribbons tied to wreaths on the doors,
Lights strung in arches from lampposts of town,
And people excitedly milling around.

It is white, fluffy masses of snow on the street,
And holiday greetings from those whom we meet.
It is children with wide eyes viewing the toys,
And people conspiring to surprise girls and boys.

Christmas is firesides and logs all ablaze,
And the stirring of memories of dear olden days;
It is sugar and spices, plum pudding and pies,
And succulent turkey stuffed to big balloon-size.

It is smells in the kitchen, where fudge simmers low,
And popcorn is popping and children's eyes glow
As bundles and boxes are placed neath the tree,
Where a rainbow of lights glows exquisitely.

Christmas is happiness, it is laughter and fun . . .
It is sharing and doing and love for each one.

Helen Shick

Some ABC's of Christmas

Alice Leedy Mason

A is holy angels
Appearing high above,
Announcing a cappella
God's wondrous gift of love.

B is lowly Bethlehem,
The birthplace of a king,
The Bible with its blessings
And bells that sweetly ring.

C means cards and candles
Are the custom of the day,
While choirs sing Christmas carols
To crowds along the way.

D stands for December,
Decorations to delight,
Dolls and drums and Doberman
Kept secretly from sight.

E says eager shepherds
Went East, led by a star,
As earnest Christians every day
Exalt Him near and far.

F stands for the frankincense
For future times foretold,
Friendship, family, faithful hearts
And the Father known of old.

G speaks of the gospel,
Good news, the gift of grace,
Of Galilee, the Magi's gold
And great old songs of praise.

H is hearth and holly,
Holidays at home,
Heavenly hosts and humble hearts
And hope for those that roam.

I is for Immanuel
And no room in the inn.
Instead He chose a stable
With peace and love within.

J is Joseph's journey
With Mary long ago,
It's jumping ropes and jerseys
And jewels to wear and show.

K is for kaleidoscopes,
For knitting (almost done),
Kitchens filled with sweets and spice,
And kittens in the sun.

L is for the laughter,
The lavender and lace,
For love that lifts the lonely heart
And lights the stranger's face.

M tells of the manger
And a mother's gentle care,
Mistletoe and miracles
And music everywhere.

N is the Nativity—
That holy night so grand.
It's navy ships and noble thoughts
And neighbors near at hand.

O stands for omnipotent—
One God for you and me.
It's oats to feed the reindeer,
Ornaments on the tree.

P means precious promise.
It's pastry to prepare.
The family plans and presents
Provide for praise and prayer.

Q . . . now that's the question!
Be quick to qualify.
It's quaint old dolls, ducks that quack
And quilts piled shoulder high.

R is for remembrance,
Relatives, rich and poor,
Gifts with bright red ribbons
And recipes galore.

S is for the Savior,
The shepherds and the song,
For sugarplums and sweetmeats
And sleighs that scoot along.

T is for the turkey
With tasty treats to try.
It's toy trains and trees to trim,
Glad tidings from on high.

U might be a unicorn
If unicorns were real.
Instead it's for unusual gifts
That have unique appeal.

V tells of the village
Where the Virgin had her child,
Of vesper bells at evening
And voices sweet and mild.

W stands for wonderful
In the good old-fashioned way,
Christmas wish and Wassail dish
And waiting for the day.

X is toy xylophones
With greetings to express,
Extending hope for health and joy
And extra happiness.

Y is a yellow sports car,
A gourmet Yuletide feast.
It's yachts and yaks and yo-yos
And sweetbreads made with yeast.

Z is for old zither tunes,
For zebras at the zoo,
A Christmas blessed with love expressed
From A to Z for YOU!

What Is Christmas?

Christmas is Music . . . the music of carols ringing out on the still night air, the organ, the chimes, and the voices of a choir singing "Silent Night, Holy Night."

Christmas is Lights . . . the candles in our windows, the lighted trees, the eyes of children, and the starlight on a cold December night.

Christmas is Welcome . . . the wreath on our door, the happiness to answer the doorbell, the warmth of hearts overflowing, "Come in, come in, and Merry Christmas."

Christmas is Laughter . . . the laughter that starts in our toes and bubbles up, the smiles on faces eveywhere, the feeling of closeness, of a wonderful secret shared with all mankind.

Christmas is Fragrance . . . the pine and spruce smell of Christmas trees, the sugary, good smell of cookies baking, the spice and raisin smell of fruitcake, the smell of furniture polish, and the cold, crisp smell of outdoors.

Christmas is Giving . . . the present made by hand, the card picked especially for a certain person, the gift marked from me to you with love.

Christmas is Remembering . . . other Christmases, friends that may be far away, loved ones far and near, those less fortunate, those in need. To read again the words "For God so loved," "Unto us a son is born."

Christmas is Love . . . the love that wells up in our hearts and brings tears to our eyes as we thank God for His great love, His unspeakable gift.

Carol Bessent Hayman

CHRISTMAS COUNTDOWN

15

14

13

16

17

18

19

20

21

22

23

24

Advent calendar courtesy of Dee Rahn.

"Gale, Bev, it's time to get up."

Two tousled heads yawn, roll over and stuff their faces deep into the pillows.

"You don't want to be late for school, do you?"

Two groans emanate from the pillows.

"I'll make you a nice, hot breakfast of oatmeal."

No response.

"Well, it's up to you, but don't forget that today is December first."

After a momentary pause, the covers fly back as two pairs of legs thrust feet into slippers and scamper off to the kitchen, robes trailing behind. Standing before what appears to be a large Christmas card tacked to the pantry door, two little girls, five years apart, debate whether age really comes before beauty.

The Advent calendar has always played an important role in my family's Christmas celebration. It made those long days between Thanksgiving and Christmas bearable by providing each day of December with its own special surprise. Every morning my sister and I opened a numbered door on the calendar, revealing some symbol of Christmas: an angel, a teddy bear, a candy cane, a candle. Even though we used the same calendar year after year, we never remembered what was hidden behind each door. And, of course, we never ever argued about whose turn it was to open the door.

Generally speaking, an Advent calendar is a large card with either twenty-four or twenty-five individual pictures, each numbered and corresponding with one of the days preceding Christmas and including Christmas Day. Most often these pictures are concealed behind flaps or doors. Sometimes they are intended for coloring day by day.

Ethnically speaking, I have never been sure just where this Christmas custom originated; my father is Dutch, my mother is German and English and the calendar we used is Scandinavian. But origins matter little when compared with this custom's significance as an integral part of my family's unique and memorable way of celebrating Christmas.

That's what counts!

Beverly Wiersum Charette

The Chimes   Erma Bombeck

Everything is in readiness.

The tree is trimmed. The cards taped to the doorframe. The boxes stacked in glittering disarray under the tree.

Why don't I hear chimes?

Remember the small boy who made the chimes ring in a fictional story years ago? As the legend went, the chimes would not ring unless a gift of love was placed on the altar. Kings and men of great wealth placed untold jewels on the altar, but year after year the church remained silent.

Then one Christmas Eve, a small child in a tattered coat made his way down the aisle and without anyone noticing he took off his coat and placed it on the altar. The chimes rang out joyously throughout the land to mark the unselfish giving of a small boy.

I used to hear chimes.

I heard them the year one of my sons gave me a tattered piece of construction paper on which he had crayoned two hands folded in prayer and a moving message, "OH COME HOLY SPIT!"

I heard them the year I got a shoebox that contained two baseball cards and the gum was still with them.

I heard them the Christmas they all got together and cleaned the garage.

They're gone, aren't they? The years of the lace doilies fashioned into snowflakes . . . the hands traced in plaster of paris . . . the Christmas trees of pipe cleaners . . . the thread spools that held small candles. They're gone.

The chubby hands that clumsily used up two dollars' worth of paper to wrap a cork coaster are sophisticated enough to take a number and have the gift wrapped professionally.

The childish decision of when to break the ceramic piggy bank with a hammer to spring the fifty-nine cents is now resolved by a credit card.

The muted thump of pajama-covered feet paddling down the stairs to tuck her homemade crumb scrapers beneath the tree has given way to pantyhose and fashion boots to the knee.

It'll be a good Christmas. We'll eat too much. Make a mess in the living room. Throw the warranties into the fire by mistake. Drive the dog crazy taping bows to his tail. Return cookies to the plate with a bite out of them. Listen to Christmas music.

But Lord . . . what I would give to bend low and receive a gift of toothpicks and library paste and hear the chimes just one more time.

From *If Life Is a Bowl of Cherries—What Am I Doing in the Pits?* by Erma Bombeck. Copyright © 1971, 1972, 1973, 1974, 1975, 1976, 1977, 1978 by Erma Bombeck. Published by McGraw-Hill Book Company. Used with permission.

Candles, fir
and fire-Glow

Candles, fir and fire-glow
Linger down the years,
Kept in memory's treasure,
Through all smiles and tears,
Prized in spite of reason,
Which would deem them small,
Ready for some moment
Of a fond recall!

Candles, fir and fire-glow,
Baubles on a tree,
Children's eyes reflecting
Everything they see . . .
These I shall remember
Till all else will fade!
Christmas is one pleasure
I would never trade!

Louise Weibert Sutton

What does a little one really see
In the fairyland of a Christmas tree
That makes big eyes shine with delight
When lights are low and the fireplace bright?
Is it angels flying there in space
Or the smile on a gingerbread man's kind face . . .
Or tinsel sparkling, all aglow,
Like diamonds shining in the snow . . .
Or the star so high in the lovely tree
It is almost hidden from one so wee?

I pray as I hold her that someway in part
Christ will be Christmas in her tiny heart . . .

George L. Ehrman

A Prayer at Christmas

This is the Gift

Songs and stories
Woven in beauty and enchantment,
Tell about wise men
Wandering far at night,
Seeking to give omen
Under radiance of starlight.

As the stars shine
And winter snows cover the earth,
Candle lights turn up
For the Christmas season,
In profusion so bright
Stillness comes over creation.

Mary Mikulski

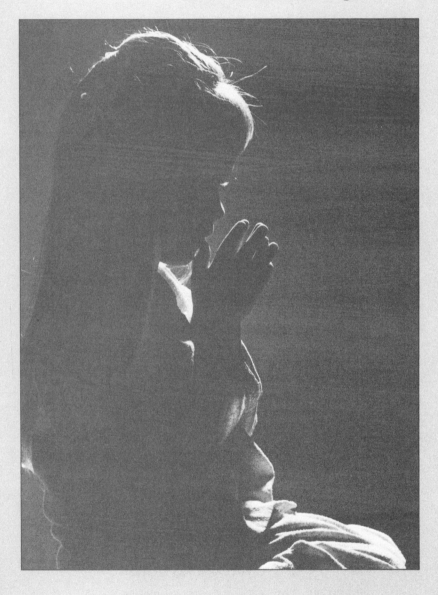

May This Be a Blessed Christmas

Cold and rugged is the north wind,
White and drifted is the snow,
But it only emphasizes,
More and more, the Christmas glow.
Snug we are, as Yule approaches;
Christmas lights and evergreen

Give the home a festive motive
That at no other time is seen,
Neighbors call and exchange greetings;
Festive boards promote good cheer;
Children wait and count the moments
As the time for gifts draws near.
And the coming of the Christ Child
Is retold and listened to
As it has been through the ages—
Ever lovely—ever new.
And our Christmas wish to your house
Calls for blessings from above
From our gracious Heavenly Father—
And from us, too—with lots of love!

James R. Lowell

Christmas Eve Moment

Adeline Roseberg

The little ones
Have gone to sleep,
There reigns a calm
That's sweet and deep.

Above the mantel
Greens entwine,
Exuding a fragrance
Of fir and pine.

The hearth-fire now
Is burning low,
The tree lights cast
A gentle glow.

Our treetop angel,
Smiling, fair,
Shines—and I kneel
In silent prayer.

Goin' Home for Christmas

Roy Lee Harmon

My heart is just so full of joy
It does a song and dance.
Plain, old, unvarnished grief and woe
Today don't have a chance.
I am goin' back, I tell you . . . yes,
In spite of snow or rain,
I'm goin' back to Mother's house
For Christmas once again.

At other times I may feel low
And all my troubles seem
A bit too much . . . but on this day
My life's a happy dream.
Oh, the wreaths are in the windows
And the tree is dressed up fine,
And I'm heading home for Christmas
With the folks that I call mine.

The house is not a palace,
But it will look good to me;
When celebrating Christmas,
Home's the only place to be.
The uncles, aunts and cousins
Will be coming in to call.
While the good old Christmas spirit
Brings some gaiety to all.

There will be some noisy chatter,
And some sad goodbyes at last,
But I'll have golden memories
To cherish when it's past.
I want to put my feet beneath
That table one more time . . .
I want to dream of days back
When life was a lilting rhyme.

A Christmas dinner when you're home
Is manna from above,
They season everything you eat—
Or say—with honest love.
Back home again for Christmas!
That is a pretty phrase;
I've carried it within my heart
For many hopeful days.

I don't care where you've settled
Or how far you've chanced to roam,
When it is time for Christmas,
That's the time to be at home.
Now may your Christmas be the best
To trip along life's lane,
And may you spend it happily . . .
With home folks once again.

IT'S CHRISTMAS

Christmas is a magic time
When all the world is bright;
It finds a place within our hearts
And fills us with delight.

The world is much more beautiful,
A richer, softer glow.
It seems that God is reaching down
To touch each soul below.

Christmas is a happiness,
A day of hope and peace,
When everyone is kind and good
And worries seem to cease.

A time of love and blessedness,
Remembrance fond and dear,
A childlike faith is ours again
This precious once a year.

Let us keep Christmas beautiful
Without a thought of greed,
That it might live forevermore
To fill our every need,

That it shall not be just a day,
But last a lifetime through,
The miracle of Christmastime
That brings God close to you.

Garnett Ann Schultz

Where Is the Christ of Christmas?

My skin felt the cold tingle as gentle flakes of new white snow fell against my face, while others created a glistening collar on my shoulders. Escaping from the noisy pre-Christmas crowds and the visual barrage of tinsel in the shopping center, I breathed a sigh of relief as I finally reached my car.

A feeling of anger and frustration filled me most of the trip home. Why had this most beautiful of Christian seasons been so obscured by things completely unrelated to the birth of Christ our Lord? Christmas specials were to be seen everywhere, as were Santa Clauses, bells, lights, candy canes, and bright packages, but there was hardly any evidence of the Christ of Christmas.

Then, quietly and gently, the Holy Spirit made me aware of the words Joseph spoke to his brothers who had sold him as a slave into Egypt, "God turned into good what you meant for evil" (Gen. 50:20 *The Living Bible*). As I thought about these words, I felt God was showing me that I should look deeper into the possibility of seeing Jesus in all those things that had upset me, yes, even those that have their origins in paganism.

Over the next few days, amid the aroma of Christmas cookies baking, I could hardly wait to find quiet moments alone with God and my Bible, so I could begin to uncover the revelation I was sure awaited me. Some Christmas symbols were much easier for me to unfold than others. Joy filled my heart and replaced the anger of previous days as the Holy Spirit helped me to see Christ where I had not been able to see Him before. Piece by piece the mystery unfolded before me.

The Christmas wreath, made of evergreens, should cause us to think of eternal life that is ours in Christ Jesus our Lord. From ancient times a wreath always symbolized a glorious victory. What could be a more glorious victory than Christ's defeat of Satan, sin and death? 1 Corinthians 15:54 states, "Death is swallowed up in victory."

Hearing Christmas bells, we can consider Psalm 100:1, "Make a joyful noise unto the Lord, all ye lands." There is little in Scripture about bells. One beautiful picture is given in Exodus 28:33-35 in the description of the elaborate pattern for the priest's robe which was to have many golden bells sewn around the hem so that the priest could be heard as he was ministering for the people in the Holy of Holies. Christmas bells could well serve to remind us of Christ, our High Priest. "He came as High Priest . . . and once for all [entered] into that inner room, the Holy of Holies . . . and . . . made sure of our eternal salvation." (Hebrews 9:11-12 *The Living Bible*).

When we see a candy cane we can think of Jesus, the Good Shepherd. Let its shape remind us of a shepherd's crook and the words of Jesus, "I am the Good Shepherd, and know my sheep, and am known of mine" (John 10:14). As the white color of the body of the cane causes us to think of the purity of Jesus, let the red stripes help us remember the blood of His sacrifice, " . . . with His stripes we are healed" (Isa. 53:5). The fragrance of peppermint is symbolic of hyssop, a bushy herb used in purification rites. David asks God, "Purge me with hyssop and I shall be clean; wash me and I shall be whiter than snow" (Ps. 51:7). As we break and share a candy cane, recall His words, "This is my body, which is broken for you" (1 Cor. 11:24).

We should try not to let Christmas gifts obscure Jesus, the best of all gifts. "For God so loved the world, that he gave his only begotten Son, that whosoever believeth in Him should not perish, but have everlasting life" (John 3:16). The gift giver: the Heavenly Father. The gift: His Son, Jesus, Savior. The recipient: anyone who accepts in faith the promise of His love and obeys His voice. As we wrap each of our gifts we can spend that time in prayer for the one who will receive it, that he might be led to a deeper relationship with Jesus.

Christmas lights are perhaps the most plentiful of all symbols. When we see these, let us remember in our hearts the words of Jesus as recorded in John 8:12, "I am the Light of the World: he that followeth me shall not walk in darkness but shall have the light of life!" As we receive this illumination from Him, we are commissioned to share it with each other, for Matthew 5:14 records that, "Ye are the light of the world."

The Christmas star is perhaps the purest object in all our Christmas symbolism, coming very directly from the Christmas story. "Where is He that is born King of the Jews? For we have seen his star in the east and are come to worship Him" (Matt. 2:2). Did you ever really notice that they didn't just come to visit, to see, but they came to worship? Let a star cause us to think beyond this star of Bethlehem to the words of Rev. 22:16, "I Jesus . . . am the root and the offspring of David, and the Bright and Morning Star."

Holly, with its prickly thorns and bright red berries can serve as a vivid reminder of the crown of thorns our Savior wore, with drops of His red blood where the berries grow. From there we can focus our thoughts on one of the crowns. He has promised His followers: "And when the Chief Shepherd shall appear, ye shall receive a crown of glory that fadeth not away" (1 Pet. 5:4).

God used these applied symbols to teach and heal me of my angry, negative feelings, and replace them with joy.

I was filled with excitement as I began to make plans for our family Christmas celebration. We daily used one of these "new" thoughts in an after-dinner time of sharing with our family. Dark-haired thirteen-year-old Kimberly lit a candle as she read about Jesus, the light of the world. Quiet, sensitive seventeen-year-old Larry unwrapped a candy cane as he shared with the family its symbolism. Our active, athletic sixteen-year-old David rang a bell for sound effects as he read to us about Christ, our high priest.

God is so wonderful. What I felt was meant for evil, He has indeed "turned into good."

Marjorie Gordon

The Christmas Story

Georgia B. Adams

Turn with me to the Bible's page,
Where we can now recall
The story of the Savior's birth—
God's gift—the King of all.

Turn with me to Matthew, where
He tells us God's dear Son
Was born in a dreary cattle stall;
That wise men, one by one,

Came from afar to bring their gifts,
To bow before His bed,
(And even now it seems we see
The halo round His head.)

Then turn over to Mark's account,
Where shepherds viewed the star
And gathered there at Bethlehem
From near and from afar.

Oh, read the story once again,
And, in our mind's eye, we
Will gather there at Bethlehem
To worship reverently!

O Little Town of Bethlehem

The voice of him that crieth in the wilderness, "Prepare ye the way of the Lord; make straight in the desert a highway for our God. Every valley shall be exalted, and every mountain and hill shall be made low; and the crooked shall be made straight, and the rough places plain; and the glory of the Lord shall be revealed, and all flesh shall see it together, for the mouth of the Lord hath spoken it."

Isaiah 40:3-5

And it shall be for a sign and for a witness unto the Lord of hosts in the land of Egypt, for they shall cry unto the Lord because of the oppressors, and he shall send them a savior, and a great one, and he shall deliver them.

Isaiah 19:20

The Prophets Foretell the Birth of Christ

Therefore the Lord himself shall give you a sign: Behold, a virgin shall conceive, and bear a son, and shall call his name *Immanuel.*

Isaiah 7:14

And the Lord gave Israel a savior, so that they went out from under the hand of the Syrians; and the children of Israel dwelt in their tents, as beforetime.

2 Kings 13:5

But thou, Bethlehem Ephratah, though thou be little among the thousands of Judah, yet out of thee shall he come forth unto me that is to be ruler in Israel; whose goings forth have been from of old, from everlasting.

Micah 5:2

The Lord thy God will raise up unto thee a Prophet from the midst of thee, of thy brethren, like unto me; unto him ye shall hearken.

Deuteronomy 18:15

For unto us a child is born, unto us a son is given; and the government shall be upon his shoulder; and his name shall be called Wonderful, Counselor, The mighty God, The everlasting Father, The Prince of Peace.

Isaiah 9:6

The Christmas Story

Now the birth of Jesus Christ was on this wise: When as his mother Mary was espoused to Joseph, before they came together, she was found with child of the Holy Ghost. Then Joseph her husband, being a just man and not willing to make her a public example, was minded to put her away privily.

But while he thought on these things, behold, the angel of the Lord appeared unto him in a dream, saying, "Joseph, thou son of David, fear not to take unto thee Mary thy wife, for that which is conceived in her is of the Holy Ghost. And she shall bring forth a son, and thou shalt call his name *Jesus*, for he shall save his people from their sins. Now all this was done, that it might be fulfilled which was spoken of the Lord by the prophet, saying, 'Behold, a virgin shall be with child, and shall bring forth a son, and they shall call his name *Emmanuel*, which being interpreted is, "God with us." ' "

Then Joseph, being raised from sleep, did as the angel of the Lord had bidden him, and took unto him his wife; and knew her not till she had brought forth her firstborn son; and he called his name *Jesus*.

Now when Jesus was born in Bethlehem of Judea in the days of Herod the king, behold, there came wise men from the east to Jerusalem, saying, "Where is he that is born King of the Jews? For we have seen his star in the east, and are come to worship him."

When Herod the king had heard these things, he was troubled, and all Jerusalem with him. And when he had gathered all the chief priests and scribes of the people together, he demanded of them where Christ should be born.

And they said unto him, "In Bethlehem of Judea, for thus it is written by the prophet, 'And thou Bethlehem in the land of Juda, art not the least among the princes of Juda, for out of thee shall come a Governor, that shall rule my people Israel.' "

Then Herod, when he had privily called the wise men, inquired of them diligently what time the star appeared. And he sent them to Bethlehem, and said, "Go and search diligently for the young child; and when ye have found him, bring me word again, that I may come and worship him also."

When they had heard the king, they departed; and, lo, the star, which they saw in the east, went before them, till it came and stood over where the young child was. When they saw the star, they rejoiced with exceeding great joy.

And when they were come into the house, they saw the young child with Mary his mother, and fell down, and worshipped him; and when they had opened their treasures, they presented unto him gifts: gold, and frankincense, and myrrh.

Matthew 1:18-2:11

A Christmas Tapestry   Paul E. Ertel

An old, dried-up sacristy in an old, dried-up church. Pastor Fulton sat at the old, dried-up desk and penciled in a few last-minute changes in his sermon. In exactly one hour the Christmas Eve Service of Holy Communion would begin, the final service of his ministry, for soon after Christmas he would leave Brudersburg to retire in a warmer climate.

There, at that beloved desk, which had been handwrought in the old country, and brought to Trinity Church in time for its day of dedication nearly two hundred years ago, he, as his predecessors, had faithfully inscribed all the parish records: births, baptisms, confirmations, weddings, membership transfers, deaths, offerings, expenditures, and all sorts of historical data.

He bowed his head and closed his eyes, and the present bowed in awe to the past, but that huge bulldozer waiting so maliciously out there beside the church forbade any thought of a future.

At the time of its founding in 1787, Trinity Church had lifted up high above Brudersburg a great inspiring cross, and this had become the landmark of the city. In recent years, however, this had been all but lost among the towering new office buildings crowding in about it.

For a century and a half this great church had provided a many-faceted ministry to the area, but with the vast expansion of the city, and the flight of so many to the suburbs, the membership had declined from a peak of more than a thousand to less than a hundred. Its once-strong Sunday School could not survive the loss of its children and young people. Its choirs, for many years the pride of Brudersburg, had long been silent. Only the willingness of its talented and dedicated organist, Helen Kirche, to play for the Sunday Services without pay kept the sound of music in the sanctuary. The once-mighty organ was frequently out of order, and on such occasions the faltering voices of its few remaining members did not contribute much to the mood of worship.

Asher, the aging sexton, who knew and loved every nook and cranny of the church, and who had always insisted that he be called the sexton rather than the janitor, the caretaker, or the custodian, had for nearly a decade provided his services purely as a labor of love.

The building was in need of extensive repair, but the small membership could in no way afford it. In fact, the church would have been without a pastor for several years had not Pastor Fulton been willing to accept whatever was to be had, including a small subsidy from The Inner City Fund of the denomination, never quite ceasing to hope that somehow the church might experience renewal.

During the early years of his ministry he had always had the manger scene with the Holy Family at the Christmas Eve Service. How often in recent weeks his memory had returned to that Christmas Eve Service thirty years before when Mary and Joseph and the Baby Jesus had made this service come alive for the last time; but even then attendance was declining.

His custom had been to invite the parents of the newest baby of the church to bring their child and serve as the Holy Family. However, during that whole year only one child had been born to a member family. Indeed, how well he remembered his coming! At one o'clock in the morning of August 1, 1948, he had been called to the hospital to baptize the newborn son of Joe and Marian Neubel, for the doctors believed that the child could not live through the night; and were he to survive at all, he was almost certain to be handicapped both physically and mentally throughout his life. The precious little boy, struggling to live, could not be removed from the special care unit in which he had been placed, so Pastor Fulton could only extend his hand momentarily into the unit, touch the little one's forehead with a tiny bit of water, and say, "Christopher Eugene Neubel, I baptize you in the name of the Father, and of the Son, and of the Holy Spirit, Amen."

Two weeks later the new mother was dismissed from the hospital, but baby Christopher, whose life was suspended as by a thread, remained there. Several weeks later he was dismissed, but the quality of his future was very uncertain. Pastor Fulton visited the Neubels every few days, and shared their joy and their concern.

Early in December Joe was notified by the company for which he worked that on February 1 of the new year he would be transferred to its office on the West Coast. This came as both a shock and a joy to the Neubels; a shock because of Christopher's health, but a joy because with the larger income, they could better care for him. All of this Joe and Marian shared with their pastor, and he was present when they made their final decision to move. "Who knows?" he said, "This may be God's way of helping both you and Christopher through these times."

Several days before Christmas, Pastor Fulton phoned the Neubels and asked if they could see him a few minutes that evening. "We certainly can," they told him. "We'll be looking for you."

A few hours later, as they sat in the Neubels' living room, Pastor Fulton said, "My visit this evening is for a very special purpose. For all the years I have been at Trinity Church I have had the parents of the newest baby in the church bring their little one and serve as the Holy Family at our Christmas Eve Service. Christopher is not only the newest baby this year, but the only one. I am inviting you to bring him to the service this Christmas Eve and serve as the Holy Family. I am aware of all the reasons you might have not to do this, but I have what I believe is a very good reason to do it."

"And what reason is that?" asked Joe.

"Yes," said Marian, "It must be a very good reason."

"I believe it is," said the pastor. "There are many ways to pray. Most of our prayers are spoken with words. Sometimes we only think our prayers. There are many symbolic ways to pray, such as kneeling, bowing the head, folding the hands, and closing the eyes. During most of my life, I have prayed by embodying my prayers in meaningful acts. Across the years I have chosen some rather difficult acts, and have lifted them up before God very much as I lift up the bread and wine at the Holy Sacrament. Many times I have felt His presence very near, and His guidance very strong.

"My invitation is to bring Christopher to this Christmas Eve Service and serve as the Holy Family, not as a favor to me, although it would be that, nor as an act of love to the church, although of course, it would be that. I suggest that you do this as an acted prayer of thanks that your little boy has survived these first difficult months; and that in this way you may share with our Father your hope that with the passing of the years, he may know all the blessings of health, happiness, and love."

The Neubels drew deep breaths and wondered what they should do.

"I shall go now," said their pastor, "and give you an opportunity to think about it. When you have made your decision, let me know."

The Neubels thought long and seriously about this. They even sought the counsel of their doctor, that they might make the proper decision. A few days later they phoned Pastor Fulton and agreed to do as he had suggested, "providing Christopher is as well on Christmas Eve as now." Their pastor thanked them warmly, for this would be a time of joy to everyone.

But all of this was now thirty years ago. His immediate concern was this, the final service of his ministry.

At the service the previous Christmas Eve the gracious old sanctuary had been host to only thirty-four people, but he had reminded them that, compared with the number at the manger in Bethlehem, they were a rather large gathering.

Since then, the Resident Bishop and his advisors had made a thorough study of Trinity Church and its problems, and had reluctantly decided that at the beginning of the next year, the building should be removed, and the ground turned over to the city to build a parking garage.

As he brooded over all this, and his retirement from the ministry, Pastor Fulton was disturbed by an urgent knocking at the sacristy door. It was Helen, the organist. She had come to the church a bit early to rehearse her music, but the organ had gone dead.

Pastor Fulton hurried to the blower room in the basement, threw off his coat and began going over the mechanism in search of the cause. The fuse and the switch were both intact, but the blower refused to work. Using such tools as were available, he searched feverishly, until half an hour later he discovered a broken wire, and working very carefully, repaired it with only a few minutes to go before the service was to begin. He ran to the kitchen to wash up, hoping to come to the Holy Sacrament with clean hands as well as a pure heart, and was rewarded with the sound of organ music coming from the sanctuary.

While Pastor Fulton was at work in the blower-room, Asher, the sexton, had noticed a special couple making its difficult way up the church steps from the cold winter night. The young mother was carrying a small baby wrapped in warm blankets. Her husband was assisted in his climb by a pair of sophisticated crutches, but as he came through the door his face was covered with perspiration, for he had made it up the steps only with great effort.

The old sexton held the door for them and welcomed them to the service. Sensing suddenly that this young family was not only burdened with

continued

a serious problem, but blessed with an incredible possibility, Asher urged them to follow him, and led them directly to the sacristy. He told them how for thirty years there had not been a Holy Family at the Christmas Eve Service. If they would consent to serve as such tonight he could supply the proper garments, for they were still intact in their leather bag in the sacristy closet. To his pleasure, they readily consented.

When Pastor Fulton finally returned to the sacristy, he noticed some coats lying on the desk, but he had not time to ask questions. Off came his coat; on went his vestments; but in his hurry he left his sermon notes lying on the desk. Whispering a prayer for guidance and strength as he moved into the sanctuary, he was completely astounded, for there sat a congregation that filled the church to the very front pew. What he didn't know was that the good Bishop had engineered a movement among all the churches of the city to send a few of their own members to this final service in Trinity Church, and the final one of Pastor Fulton's ministry. The Bishop himself was present, having placed additional bread and wine upon the altar, but Pastor Fulton was too excited to notice this.

To his amazement, only a few feet in front of the altar stood the manger he had made so many years ago with his own hands; and lying in it was a tiny baby, moving its arms and legs and making all the sounds for which little ones are so much loved. About this Holy Family, however, there was something different. Mary was standing at the Manger, and Joseph was sitting; and on the floor at his side lay a pair of crutches.

Under the leadership of Pastor Fulton, the music and scripture of the Nativity blended with the time-honored liturgy of the Sacrament. When it was time for the sermon, instead of going to the pulpit, Pastor Fulton went over to the Manger and stood just back of Mary and Joseph where he could see the Baby Jesus. Then looking out toward this incredible congregation, he said, "First of all, I want to thank all of you for coming to this service. I don't know how your coming was arranged, but I can never thank you enough, and especially those who asked you to come. Second, as I bring my ministry to a close, I shall always remember with joy beyond words, that you have come, and that at long last I have had once more a Holy Family at the Christmas Eve Service. And third, I do not know these wonderful people who are Mary and Joseph, and the Baby Jesus. I do not know how they came to be here, but I cannot escape the conviction that somehow the hand of God is present in this!"

At this point, though totally out of character, Joseph turned toward the old pastor, and said, "Pastor Fulton, I know this is very unusual, but may I say just a few words?"

"Please do," replied the pastor.

"Very well," continued the young man. "I hold here in my hand my Baptismal Certificate signed by Pastor George M. Fulton on August 1, 1948; and I am the son of Joe and Marian Neubel, members of Trinity Church until they were moved to the West Coast almost thirty years ago. And this," pointing to Mary, "is my wife, Jennie; and the Baby Jesus is our baby boy of three months, George Fulton Neubel.

"My beloved parents were married by Pastor Fulton at this very altar; and when I was born here at Brudersburg, the doctors told them that I might not live through the night. I was put into a special care unit, and Pastor Fulton was called to the hospital to baptize me. The doctors said that even if I were to live, I would probably be handicapped both physically and mentally. As you can see, I am handicapped physically, and without these crutches I would have to move about in a wheelchair. However, I am otherwise in excellent health; and thanks to God, and to my wonderful parents who still live in health and happiness on the West Coast, I was able to graduate from the University and the Conservatory of Music. My family and I have come back to Brudersburg because I have accepted a position as first violinist with the Brudersburg Symphony, beginning the middle of January. Before Pastor Fulton goes to his new home in the south, Jennie and I want him to baptize our infant son, his namesake."

With that, the young man resumed his role as Joseph, and no one could ever recall a Holy Family so reverent and beautiful.

Very quietly the Bishop came to the front of the church, and without saying a word, assisted the pastor with the bread and wine.

Finally, before sending the people forth with the Peace of Christ, Pastor Fulton and the good Bishop knelt in silent prayer at the altar. While they knelt there each of them felt a hand laid gently upon his shoulder. Concluding their prayer, they looked up, and there stood the young musician. His hands were trembling. Tears were streaming from his eyes. Through his tears a great light was shining. But his crutches were lying on the floor beside the manger!

A Study
in Contrast

Priceless stained-glass windows
Paint rainbows on the snow,
While within the great cathedral
An organ plays soft and low.

Pews pillowed soft for comfort
Hold leather-bound songs of praise,
As silver-held tapers indulge in
Waxen wonders and shadow plays.

There, just below the altar,
On harsh and prickly hay,
In a manger crude and lowly,
The sleeping Christ Child lay.

Unaware of surrounding grandeur,
Those of faith pass by this night,
To recall the humble beginning of
The Way, The Truth, and The Light.

Lois J. Martinec

Hope and Joy

Herald angels, come and sing,
Tell the world a child is king,
Prince of heaven, Lord of earth,
Sing a song of Jesus' birth.

Sturdy shepherds, leave your shee[p]
Come and see the Babe asleep,
Safe and warm in Mary's arms,
Unaware of future harms.

Learned Wise Men from afar,
Hear the message, see the star,
Find the Babe so long foretold.
Bring Him incense, myrrh and gold.

Patient Joseph, watch with care
Mary and the Baby there.
Keep them safe throughout the night,
Soon will come the morning light.

Gentle Mary, love's begun.
You have borne God's only Son,
Earth and heaven's hope and joy
Wrapped up in your baby boy.

Mary K. Rabb

Kindred Souls

From those who were shepherds
To wisest of mortals,
Strangers came streaming
From near and afar—

The peasants so lowly,
The royal so mighty:
Determinedly following
Light from the star.

In awed adoration,
They knelt by the manger;
Strangers, but bound
In devotion as one—

The peasants so lowly,
The royal so mighty:
Each equal in God's sight.
Each heart held His Son.

Dorothy I. Neel

God's Corner

Clasp Christmas close to you. Hold it fast in your embrace so that the billowing fogs of prejudice, disdain, and indifference so sadly prevalent in much of today's thinking can in no way deprive you of its wondrous beauty. I am not talking about the commercially accepted concept of Christmas; I am talking about the old-fashioned, almost outmoded concept of the spirit of Christmas.

Suppose you could not afford to buy gifts for your family and friends. Would that deprive you of celebrating Christmas? Is Christmas a mere exchange of gifts? Were the Wise Men commercially-minded when they traveled a great distance to bring the finest they possessed to the Christ Child, or did they see beyond the visible to the infinite the child symbolized? Did they kneel in homage to a human being or in awe to a vision?

Must today's technological age be permitted to deprive us of the faith upon which Christianity has been built? Is faith not a substance of things hoped for, the evidence of things not seen? Can we afford to cast aside the only Power and Presence upon which we can rely for safe conduct through a maze of bewildering digressions in the field of the spiritual? Are the three Wise Men being replaced by the seven theologians who recently professed to have discovered the truth about Jesus, the man?

Christmas is an individual matter. To some it may be walking through snow-laden streets to a midnight mass, with its candlelight procession dispelling the darkness of human beliefs, its chorus of richly blended voices proclaiming the birth of a Savior, "For unto you is born this day in the city of David a Savior, which is Christ the Lord."

For some it might be a Christmas oratorio—massed choruses, glorious arias, and a supporting orchestral accompaniment, all combining to erase the pressures of the world as one is enfolded in the joy of the spirit.

For some it may be the happiness of the family drawn together in love of one another and of the special occasion they are celebrating. Surely nothing can exceed the joy of Christmas when a father and mother and their children and children's children come together to commemorate the birth of the Christ with Christmas gifts, a gaily decorated tree, laughter and, above all, a conscious awareness of the real meaning of Christmas.

If you are among those fortunate enough to have Christmas in your heart, take a few seconds on Christmas Eve to step out-of-doors and search the heavens for a star, one that shines more brilliantly than do the others. You will find, as you gaze intently upward, that it makes contact with you. It says, reassuringly, "Be not afraid. All is well. I am the star the Wise Men followed. I am the star the world will once again hold fast in its embrace because I am the star that leads to the Christ Child. Just follow me."

Gertrude M. Puelicher

No Room at the Inn

Katherine Markowitz

Once, two thousand years ago,
On a clear and starlit night,
Shepherds who kept their sheep in the hills
Saw a vision of unearthly light.

The birth of a Baby Boy was foretold
Who would save His people from sin;
But when His parents came to a Judean town,
They found there no room at the inn.

So Jesus was born in a stable that eve.
A treasure was He of great worth,
Yet He was born there among the animals,
A majesty of majesties on earth.

His parents were humble sojourners.
They were tired and hungry and poor,
But there could no warm room be found for them,
Just a cold, straw-strewn stable floor.

Jesus came to live among men,
A lovely stranger from celestial parts.
I pray we might all find room for Him
This night at the inn of our hearts.

And she brought forth her firstborn
son, and wrapped him in swaddling
clothes, and laid him in a manger;
because there was no room for them in
the inn.

Luke 2:6-7

The Gift

Electricity—necessity, convenience, or luxury? I smile a bit as I read this question. To our family, electric power was none of these—when it came, it simply came as a gift.

I was born in the middle of the Depression in Darrington, Washington, a small logging town. For thirty-five years we lived in the same big house about three miles from town. For twenty-five years of that time, it was without electricity.

We lived not on "the wrong side of the tracks," but on "the wrong side of the river." Electricity didn't exist for us, although the townspeople had it. Strange as it may seem, I can't remember missing it at all—not then! We pumped our water, chopped our wood, and were happy.

There are many memories from those days. Often it is a simple thing that takes me back for a moment to a way of life that is gone forever. Recently someone on television quoted part of the famous "Charge of the Light Brigade." It brought to mind one of the most memorable days of those years—the day electrical power came to "our side of the river."

It was the day for which we had waited, prepared, hoped.

Waiting our turn, we watched one of the local electricians cut funny holes in the walls, drop cords, and install those magic boxes that would in time replace our big kerosene and Aladdin lamps. We were ready.

Then it came—*the day*! We had the honor of having a large transformer on a pole out by the road in front of our place. It was a dead giveaway. From early morning until dark, our home was overrun—with vacuum cleaner salesmen! They must have almost bumped into each other going from home to rural home, striking at the exact moment calculated to catch prospective customers receptive to their electrical wonders!

We had already purchased a vacuum cleaner from an old acquaintance; but as the procession continued Dad decided to have some fun. He was working outside near the entrance to our long driveway when a car drove in, stopped, and the salesman asked, "Is the lady of the house at home?" Dad could see the vacuum cleaners in his back seat.

"Yes, she is," Dad said solemnly. "But if you could see what she and my daughter just did to the last three vacuum salesmen who were here, you wouldn't ask!" The man backed his car from the driveway, throwing gravel in his haste, and disappeared down the road!

At last *the day* gave way to *the moment*!

"Turn 'em on!" the power company man yelled. We were poised, Mom, my brothers and I, each at a switch. In a glorious flood, there was light!

The power company man had his own sense of humor. "Mr. Reece," he said, "you might liken this to a great day in history. Here comes the charge of the light brigade!"

My father was looking at the bill for several hundred dollars, which had just been presented. Mom, the boys and I heard his reply, "Yes, and oh, what a charge they made!"

We roared. Even the power company man laughed as he climbed in his truck and went on to bring the gift of light to our next neighbor.

Unlike those who rushed out and went into debt to purchase all kinds of electrical appliances, our family did not. It took time for the old-fashioned hand pump to give way to an electric one. It took a longer time for the gas-motored Maytag, with its long, spiral exhaust we nicknamed the "Taily-Po" and which had to be put out the door to get rid of the smoke and fumes even in the coldest weather, to be converted to an electric motor. Toasters and waffle irons were not everyday purchases for us, but Christmas gifts. My parents had lived through the Depression, feeling the burden of unpaid bills. Never again! Not even for conveniences.

Perhaps we appreciated our "gift" more because of this. Every single item we had was planned for, worked for, and eagerly welcomed by all. Now we could have running water inside our home. A bathroom. A water heater, instead of great copper boilers heated on the old cookstove. And, at last, a gleaming white electric range! It took time to assimilate them into our way of life—Mom swore for years she couldn't bake a decent biscuit in that range, the way she had in her old wood stove!

Today, as I sit in an electrically heated room, using an electric typewriter and a three-way electric desk lamp, I appreciate these things a great deal—more, perhaps, than many who have had them "forever." I will finish my letter, go to the kitchen, prepare toast, maybe eggs and bacon, even orange juice—all electrically. Because I look on electric power as a gift, I am careful to turn off the lights and heat in the room I leave; shut off the stove when I am through; snap off the stereo when we are not around to hear it. For in my memory is that special day long ago when the gift of power came "across the river."

It brought a rural family a little relief from hard work, better light to read, the luxury of all the hot water we wanted. It also brought the joy and wonder of electric Christmas tree lights for the very first time. A porch light, and a yard light, and all the wonderful things we had seen in other homes and yards.

"Here comes the charge of the light brigade!" I can only add—may we always meet it joyously, appreciating the great gifts it represents. May we use them wisely, knowing they must be shared by many. May we never treat them lightly, take them for granted, or waste them. If every person could spend many years without the benefits of electrical power, perhaps there would be a greater appreciation for this great gift—as there is for me.

Colleen L. Reece

Merry Christmas

and a Happy New Year

from all of us at Ideals . . .

- In this season for Giving, what better way to remember your loved ones than by a gift subscription to Ideals?
- Continue the joy of this season throughout the year with eight beautiful issues embodying the traditional values and heritage of the American way of life that we all enjoy.
- Ideals will always bring you the finest in prose, poetry and photography. Each issue is a keepsake to be treasured . . . without the clutter and distractions of advertising.
- Ideals *Valentine* issue will bring a world of lasting beauty to you or to others that you love. Let Ideals say "Happy New Year" for you throughout the coming year!

Open the Door
to Christmas

When sleigh bells tinkle in the lane,
And warm-clad carolers make their rounds,
Open your door to Christmas,
Welcome its happy sounds.

When Yule logs blaze upon the hearth,
And kitchens scent the air with spice,
And holly hangs on your festive door,
Christmas smells so nice.

Outside your door is a Christmas wreath,
And colored lights twinkle on every tree.
People are smiling and pleasant,
Christmas is lovely to see.

Open your door to this Christmas,
To its color, its goodness, its tone.
Take Christmas into your home and heart
And make it your very own.

Mabel Jones Gabbott

Now is the time to get ready for Christmas. All year long I find things that just suit one person or another and tuck them away in cartons. So, the first problem is locating the filled cartons, which inevitably have vanished. One difficulty is that Stillmeadow was built in 1690 and nobody paid any attention to closets in those days; they stored everything in chests. That means eight chests to rummage through to find where all those August gifts were carefully laid away. Last year, one box of gifts turned up in January under a mattress pad in the maple room!

Another problem is that as I shop during the year I have sudden inspirations about gifts that just fit certain dear people. But now I have everything piled on the big four-poster, with the help of Amber, the Abyssinian, and I cannot remember who it was that mentioned in July how

Letter from Home

Gladys Taber

much she needed a new evening bag! Somehow, in the end, the gifts will get wrapped and have the right tags on them. I'll carry the carton of extra tissue paper to the woodshed, wondering why it seems so heavy. There is always a good reason. Five pounds of kitten is usually under the wrapping!

Last August I bought a special dolls' house on Cape Cod for my granddaughters. It was built by a neighbor and looked very much like Stillmeadow—slanted roof, shutters and white siding. When I got it back to the farm, we realized there was no place to keep it until Christmas. Alice and Anne would find it! So it will stay in the car trunk until the night before Christmas. Very late Christmas eve, my son-in-law, Curt, will haul it in through the snow. I've decided something smaller would be more practical for next year.

The children still hang up their stockings, and so does Amber. We open presents after breakfast, but the girls get up at daybreak to "do the stockings," as Anne says. This is an excellent plan for families with young children, and I highly recommend it to

parents who have been up half the night wrapping last-minute packages.

We have a tradition which involves playing Christmas music most of the morning. Perhaps the most important part of Christmas is in that one word—tradition. A family pattern for the holiday reaffirms that the family is a unit, and that some things in this confusing world really do remain the same. We all need an anchor, a hold on the familiar. I am always happy when Connie, my daughter, tells Alice and Anne about the special tiny angel in an eggshell made for us by a Russian friend when Connie was very young. And just which cocker puppy broke one piece of the spun-glass star that goes at the top of the tree.

Sometimes Alice dashes into my room to say, "Gram, where are those Dickens' *Carol* figures? I can't find them!" Then we locate them, packed in tissue and as lovely as they were before Alice was born. I notice Alice and Anne want everything in exactly the same place: the huge Christmas candle in the front window so people can see it; the tiny angels on the mantel where they catch the glow of

the firelight; the bayberry tapers on the trestle table. "There," says Anne grandly. "I think we are accommodated now."

Most of Christmas day neighbors drop in and the children go down to see if they can skate on the pond. If not, they go into the woods to look for deer and bobcat tracks. Secret, our house skunk, has to have a waddle in the snow, all the winter birds must be fed, and the stray cats that board at Stillmeadow need an extra holiday meal out by the old well house. And then, suddenly, dusk falls, quick and still, and the first star lights her own candle in the deepening sky.

As I reflect on Christmas, I remember why we are really celebrating this holiday. We are grateful for the birth of a simple man who never led an army or ruled a country. But He has had more influence than any ruler who ever lived, and the continent He talked about is mightier than any. He shared His world of the spirit where one loved one's neighbor. It is good to think of this as we say good night and snuff the candles again.

Deck the Halls

With Christmas Spirit

Bea Bourgeois

Some people drape a few strands of garland on the mantel, hang a wreath on the front door, and consider their homes decorated for the Christmas season.

They would probably be astonished to learn that my husband begins his holiday decorating every year on the day after Thanksgiving and takes at least a week of vacation early in December so that he can merrily deck our halls.

I don't know anyone who enjoys the Christmas season more than Bob does. Decorating is not only a hobby with him; it's a month-long labor of love, and the end result is magnificent. We store dozens of cardboard boxes in the attic, holding carefully wrapped Christmas items that we've collected through the years. There are antique glass ornaments, Christmas postcards, papier-maché Santas and Father Christmas figures, twirly metal icicles, and real tinsel—the prewar kind made of lead, not the current plastic variety. Once we begin bringing the boxes downstairs, the Christmas spirit comes right along with them.

Even the powder room is decorated for the season. Bob uses a small dab of plastic adhesive to put the old, turn-of-the-century postcards on the walls. Many of them feature bright red velvet poinsettias and bunches of holly blooming amid the tender sentiments. On one wall Bob hangs a poster from the World War II era, featuring a smiling Santa Claus advising everyone to buy United States savings bonds and stamps.

Each year the top of our upright piano becomes a miniature replica of Bethlehem. Bob covers the top with a wide strip of brown felt, and places the manger in the center. Figures carved from olive wood approach the crib; there are wise men and shepherds, and camels in single file but joined by small metal chains to form a procession. A choir of porcelain angels stands to one side.

Bob spends hours patiently hanging small silver and gold ornaments above the crib scene. Each ball hangs on a strand of nearly invisible thread which is attached to the ceiling with tiny bits of plastic adhesive. The lengths of the strings are staggered so that when all the balls are hung the scene resembles a miniature grouping of planets in the heavens.

Perhaps the most ingenious touch—people quite literally gasp in astonishment when they see it—is the Christmas Wall Bob designed. He invented the wall because we had run out of space to display all the cards we receive each year, and it has become an annual holiday tradition in our dining room.

The background is made of strands of red and green yarn, attached to eye screws on the moldings at the top and bottom of the wall. Bob threads the yarn from bottom to top in alternating colors until it forms hundreds of diamond-shaped pockets. Each individual diamond is tied with a short piece of yarn to provide enough tension so that decorations can be hung.

It takes a full day to string the yarn onto the wall, and one evening to tie all the diamonds, with everybody in the family sharing the job. Then the fun begins. Boxes are opened and trinkets unwrapped; the wall features delightful holiday items our sons made during their grade school years, miniature brass musical instruments, Victorian slipper ornaments, and hundreds of small stuffed animals—including a marvelous felt mouse dressed in the red and white robes of a Cardinal and named, appropriately, "Church Mouse." There are felt soldier boys and teddy bears, giraffes and gingerbread boys, and tiny handmade sleighs and stars. When all the decorations are hung, we add the Christmas cards by hanging them on strands of red and green yarn.

As a child I collected Storybook Dolls—pretty little bisque people dressed as nursery rhyme characters, or brides, or Mexican senoritas. The dolls also come down from the attic every Christmas; Bob stands them on the arches between the living room and dining room for a whimsical touch of toyland.

The window seat in our dining room is transformed each holiday season into a winter village, complete with a miniature church, several small buildings, and a mirrored "skating pond." Bob and the boys set up part of our old electric train set on a piece of plywood covered with green carpet tiles. The tracks run along the outside edge of the board, and "snow" (from a box of Ivory Flakes) is sprinkled on the entire scene.

There is a lighted station house, a miniature lead goose on the "pond," a celluloid duck standing imperiously in the town square, and a hand-crocheted schoolhouse that was made by a friend especially for the tableau. The train chugs through the winter night, complete with crossing gates that raise and lower and a stop at the barrel factory in the corner. Young visitors are absolutely fascinated with the old lighted Pullman cars and the stern station master who raises and lowers his arm as the train chugs past.

Bob has saved nearly everything the boys made when they were small, so each year some familiar items appear again. When the boys were young and the excitement of the season made them fidgety, we kept them occupied making decorations out of paper plates. They cut out small animals, trees, flowers, and people from old Christmas cards and glued them to paper plates, sometimes adding sequins and glitter. Each year the plates are displayed on the doors of our kitchen cabinets, and each year they become more precious.

Our sons have become steeped in holiday traditions, particularly where the Christmas tree is concerned; they are appalled at the thought of buying an artificial tree. Every year our tree stands a majestic eight or nine feet tall, and it is dressed most elegantly in garland, strings of popcorn, and hundreds of ornaments, mostly antique. Every year Bob puts on the lights and the boys hang the ornaments; we sip eggnog and listen to Christmas carol records, and we dare not deviate from this well-established routine.

The outside of our house looks almost as pretty as the inside during the month of December. Bob and the boys have strung hundreds of miniature white lights on a stately cedar tree in our front yard, and the cherry tree in the backyard wears several strings of large colored lights. In each window there are electric candelabras with three candles apiece; on a dark winter night the house looks as though it belongs in a small Austrian village. On the front porch Bob hangs a huge three-foot round wreath that he made several years ago out of pinecones and nuts.

Friends look forward to a holiday visit so they can admire the painstaking detail and the beautiful decorations that make our house a December delight. When they marvel at the amount of patience it all takes, Bob smiles and says, simply, "I just love Christmas."

Christmas Bells

Every year at Christmas
I hear them once again . . .
The merry sounds of sleigh bells
O'er the hill and glen.

Bells jingled on the harness,
And chimed upon the hills
As through the countryside we sped . . .
There was no greater thrill!

We waved to all the neighbors
As we journeyed into town,
And joined our voices with the bells
While snow came drifting down.

There are bells in great cathedrals
With their spires that reach the sky,
And radiant stained-glass windows
That only gold can buy.

There are bells in country churches
Which are nestled in the hills,
Where many a weary traveler's heart
With sweet contentment fills.

From lovely handbell choirs
Resounding music rings,
And as the children ring their bells
Their happy voices sing.

These bells are very special
With the happiness they bring,
But oh, to be a child tonight!
And hear the sleigh bells ring!

Marion Olson

Elizabeth Searle Lamb

What began as a professional career in music has developed, for our Yuletide poet, into a life-style as a successful writer. Born and raised in Topeka, Kansas, Elizabeth Searle obtained her music degree from the University of Kansas and became a professional harpist. Marriage to F. Bruce Lamb, however, took her away from her music—to the tropical forests of Latin America, where she and her husband were often the only English-speaking people for miles. Because it was impossible to take her harp along, she began to write—first prose for music, travel and inspirational magazines, and then poetry. After returning to the United States, Mrs. Lamb became interested in writing haiku and, for a year, held the office of president in the Haiku Society of America. Mrs. Lamb's poetry can be found in several haiku magazines as well as many inspirational and poetry magazines. Her writing has received numerous awards and also appears in many foreign countries. Several new books of poetry will soon be added to her current list. Presently living in what she describes as "a very old adobe house on a dirt street" in Santa Fe, New Mexico, Mrs. Lamb writes faithfully every day, yet still finds time to lead workshops and give poetry readings.

Count One, at Christmas

Count one—
One star it was
That lit the sky
That night and drew
Shepherd and king.

Count one—
One baby it was
They came to see
And stayed
To love and worship.

Count one—
One gift of love
Never diminishing,
Still shining
As it did that night;
One gift of love.

Count one, then
Reach out and take
It for your own.
It is God's gift,
Gift of love—
Gift of life!

My Resolution

Into the new year I take the power
Of prayer to order my days, indeed,
My life, into a pattern of progress.

Into the new year I take the joy
Of adventuring to lift the routine
Into a challenge of increasing
Achievement.

Kaleidoscope

Hold to your eye
The colors of Christmas:
Flame of poinsettia, holly's red,
Spicy greens and the candles' glow,
Bright papers and ribbons,
A hundred cards,
And a cathedral's hushed, dim nave.

Hold to your ear
The sounds of the season:
Christmas carols from a dozen lands,
Joyous bells and their pealing,
Organ and choir and a child's high voice,
The silence of snowfall late at night.

Hold to your heart, oh, hold to your heart,
The unchanging dream of Christmas:
The shining star that led wise men on
To a Babe in his mother's arms,
And, all about, the angels praying
As we must pray, as we all must pray,
"Peace on earth; good will to all men."

Christmas Prayer

Dear God,
Let starshine
Light each heart.
Let peace line
The humble crib.
Let love enfold
This Holy Child,
His story told
By angel choir.
Oh, let all on earth
Together lift
Adoration for this,
Thy greatest gift.
Amen.

Christmas Mobile

Hang a Christmas mobile
High, where it will catch
Firelight and sunshine:
Two silver balls,
A golden bird,
Mistletoe spray
And a shining star.
And, in the heart
The mobile's counterpart:
Love for the Christ Child—
And for all men everywhere,
Compassion,
A measure of joy,
And a constant prayer
For peace.

Song For December

Christmas
Is a caroling:
Love,
The melody
Embellished
With grace notes
Of remembrance . . .
The joy-wrapped gift,
The simple card . . .
And underneath,
The full, rich chords
Of peace on earth,
Good will to men.

To a Friend

Dear friend, I pray you well!
Into the inner silence
I carry your name, your need.
In that secret inner place
I see you, vibrant and alive,
Radiant in the glowing light.
I feel the warmth of love
That is a cloak of protection
Wrapping you about with safety
Wherever you may be.
There, in that center of stillness,
I speak your name and I hear
The echoes of assurance.
Dear friend, I pray you well!
. . . And who is not my friend?

Christmas Sampler

The evergreen bough
And the red-berried holly,
A sheaf of wheat,
A bluebird, wings outstretched,
And a garland of flowers
Tied with a ribbon of gold . . .
All the symbols
Carved in the cloth,
Stitch by loving stitch,
To frame the motto:
All glory be to God
And on the earth be
Peace to men of good will.

The Christmas Light

Radiant, the holy, singing light
Streams forth to bless on Christmas night
With some new pulse of energy . . .
Or is it only that we see
With clearer vision at this time
When we have always seen the sign
Of Christ, the Baby, born again
Within the seeking hearts of men?
This is the light that blazed the sky
When shepherds scanned the heavens high
Above their flock-filled greening hills
And heard the angels sing their trills
Of glorious glad tidings sent
Unto all men, that God had spent
The price of His own dear-loved Son
Forevermore to teach the one
Commandment, teach the law of love.
Oh, let us look, not high above
In starry skies, this Christmas night,
But in our hearts, for the Christmas light.

For one magic evening, with the moon shining on the glistening mantle of fresh-fallen snow, the main street of Nantucket belongs to people, not cars. Lighted Christmas trees, decorated with ropes of cranberries, pinecones, and handmade ornaments, line the street, standing like sentinels outside Nantucket's quaint shops.

"We wish you a merry Christmas, we wish you a merry Christmas," the carolers sing out in their brightly colored knit caps and heavy mufflers as they stroll along cobblestoned Main Street.

This scene is repeated yearly on the first weekend of December—usually on a Friday, but this year on Saturday, December 8—as a celebration that signals the start of Yuletide on the small island thirty miles off the Massachusetts coast. As if insulated by its geographical location against the modern commercialization of Christmas, Nantucket stands apart.

Carolers sing, wreaths adorn Federal doorways, and the main street is for people, not cars, during Yuletide on the island of Nantucket

Its observance of the season is quaint and low-key, a yesteryear kind of Christmas, reminiscent of a time when living was more leisurely and pleasures simple.

First settled in 1659 by Quakers, Nantucket was a stronghold of this sect for more than a century. The early houses, sheathed in silvery-gray shingles, reflect the Quaker influence. They are simple, austere dwellings with no signs of ostentation, constructed that way to discourage any show of material wealth.

By the end of the eighteenth century, however, the Federal style of architecture, so popular on the mainland, began to make its way to the island. In the center of town, houses became larger and central hallways appeared. Ceilings became higher and entrances more important with the addition of sidelights and pilasters. Windowpanes became larger and fewer in number. The island has more than four hundred dwellings virtually frozen architecturally. They range from simple late seventeenth century lean-to structures to the imposing Greek Revival mansions built on Upper Main Street during the golden age of whaling.

But it was not until the second quarter of the

nineteenth century, when Nantucket was enjoying its greatest prosperity as a whaling center and commercial seaport, that true architectural elegance was seen on the island. Stately mansions were built on Upper Main Street in the 1830s and 1840s by wealthy shipowners and whaling merchants. The best known of these are the "Three Bricks," identical brick mansions at 93, 95, and 97 Main Street, commissioned by Joseph Starbuck—an erstwhile butcher who became one of the island's most successful whaling merchants—for his three sons, William, Matthew, and George.

Then came July 13, 1846 and The Great Fire, which destroyed a third of the town. The island was still struggling to recover from that disaster when its whaling industry was dealt a fatal blow in 1855 by the discovery of methods to refine crude oil for illumination.

The island population dwindled as many of its

Old-Fashioned Island Christmas

inhabitants were forced to move to the mainland in search of jobs. Nantucket became a drowsy, depressed community just as the rest of the nation started to enjoy the newfound prosperity of the industrial age with all the embellishments of the Victorian era.

Nantucketers, unable to afford these extravagances, had to forego all the gingerbread and froufrou of the Victorian period. But this turned out to be a blessing in disguise: The island's old homes remained in their original state for the most part, preserving a rich heritage of pristine architecture in this country. Many houses fell into disrepair during the decades that followed, but they have since been restored, often by "off-islanders," or summer residents.

The off-islanders, succumbing in increasing numbers over the years to Nantucket's charm, have helped to extend the summer season past Labor Day and well into fall. Some now remain on the island through the Christmas season. Others come "home" for the holidays, flying in from winter residences as far away as Florida and Arizona to enjoy Nantucket's old-fashioned observance of Yuletide.

© 1979 Antiques News Association. Reprinted by permission of *Antiques World*, 122 East 42nd Street, New York, N.Y. 10168.
For subscription information see acknowledgment page.

Virginia Bohlin
Photographs opposite by Mark Sexton

Bayberries
—Our Fragrant Heritage

"Light ye all the candles and burn them brightly, too. If burned to the socket they'll bring wealth to the pocket and joy through the year to you."

Come Thanksgiving and Christmas, bayberry is to the nostrils what roast turkey is to the palate! Bayberry is America's traditional scent of the holidays, and most women by now are beginning their annual collections of bayberry candles.

As those candles burn, history will float through our rooms on their fragrance. For the bayberry is so distinctively American that the botanists named it *Myrica pensylvanica*—the myrtle of Pennsylvania.

The bayberry, or wax myrtle, gave much to the inhabitants of its namesake state. Colonial muskets were greased with bayberry oil to protect the metal from the weather and salt air. Flat irons were greased with "bean-bags" stuffed with bayberries and bay leaves. In trunks, drawers and chests, the leaves themselves were used as sachets; in cooking, they were seasonings. Colonists even used the leaves in dog beds as aromatic deodorizers and pesticides!

But then, as now, the greatest gift of the bayberry bush was candles.

They were welcome respites from the grayish tallow candles of the time—evil smelling things, which sputtered with uneven and feeble light, smoked thickly and coated whole rooms with sticky carbon.

Spicy freshness

You can imagine why the colonists prized the bayberry candles and used them at Thanksgiving, Christmas and other special occasions. They burned with steady blue flames, scented rooms with spicy freshness and were clear shades of olive green.

By the mid-1700s the candles had found their way deep into American tradition. A now familiar couplet from the Cape Cod area of Massachusetts expressed the new sentiment exactly:

"A bayberry candle
burned to the socket
Brings luck to the house
and gold to the pocket."

Actually, the candles brought gold only to the pockets of those itinerant chandlers who appeared in the 1800s. These colonial candlemakers set out in early autumn to make dippings to order for the wealthier housewives. They suspended more than a hundred wicks from their wheel-like "trees" which revolved slowly over the dipping kettle of hot wax.

Women made candles

Obtaining bayberry candles was a far more laborious process for the less fortunate colonial wives; they had to make their own. And their methods up until the late eighteenth century were those of the earliest pilgrims.

Timing the annual trek was vital. Colonists had to wait until a few frosts had "ripened" the berries, killed off most insects and removed at least some of the leaves. On the other hand, they had to get to the bushes before the hungry birds did!

They picked quickly, stripping off the berries by running their hands along the fruit-laden branches. Any blackened or discolored berries were discarded; such culls would lower the color quality of the candles.

When the bayberry harvest was brought home, it was carefully picked over for leaves, twigs and other foreign matter. After the cleaned berries had been placed in deep kettles, covered with cold water and placed over a fireplace—preferably, an outdoor fireplace—any remaining debris floated to the surface and was skimmed off.

As the kettle warmed, the wax melted, rose and floated on top of the water as a greenish oil. It was stirred constantly and carefully kept at a temperature cool enough to prevent aromatic volatiles from boiling away.

In about three hours, the kettle was removed from the fire. When the wax had cooled to a solid cake which floated on the water, it was carefully removed, then melted again in a smaller kettle and strained through four thicknesses of cheesecloth. The result was a chunk of pure bayberry wax.

Twenty-five dips

Dipping the candles was the next step, and preparations for it included a thorough job of housecleaning. Floors and objects in the dipping area had to be so clean that any spilled wax could be scraped loose and remelted!

The basic dipping procedure was simply to tie wicks of the proper length to sticks and dip the strings into containers of molten wax. It was tricky business! Each of the twenty-five dips required per average-size candle was imperiled by room temperature, wax temperature and the amount of wax in the kettle.

If the room was too cold, the candles cracked; if the room was too warm, the drying time per dip seemed endless.

The finished candles were brittle, and even storage was a problem. In fact, the special candle boxes and candle drawers the colonists built into their hutches and credenzas now make these pieces of furniture highly prized as antiques.

Fortunately—or unfortunately, depending on how sentimental you are—the brittle pure bayberry candles are no longer commercially available. The bayberry candles we buy at this time of the year are usually ordinary candles coated with but a few layers of bayberry wax.

Genuine tradition

Often that coating is a synthetic that simulates the rich scent and color of bayberry. If the coating is genuine, it is diluted by at least ten percent paraffin. And it is rarely the product of *Myrica pensylvanica*, for most such wax is imported from related species native to Central and South America or to South Africa.

But although those bayberry candles you light during the holidays may be imported or even synthetic, their tradition will be genuine. For bayberry candles on November 21 and December 25 are as distinctly American . . . as Thanksgiving Day and Santa Claus!

Evelyn Witter

A Long-Ago Christmas

In memory I clearly see
A Christmas Day of long ago,
When I was just a little lad
And Christmas held a magic glow.

I recall the tree in the parlor,
With candles by the score;
There were holly wreaths and mistletoe
Hung on every waiting door.

I see the firelight's flicker,
And stockings in a row;
I hear the crunch of footsteps
On diamond-studded snow.

I hear the sound of carolers,
Their merry voices singing;
I hear the sound of sleigh bells
And joyous church chimes ringing.

Yes, a Christmas Day of long ago
Held a very special joy
And brings back happy memories
When I was just a boy.

Becky Jennings

An Old-Fashioned Christmas

How I yearn for an old-fashioned Christmas
Like we had in the long, long ago,
A pine-scented tree from the forest,
Sprinkled with tinsel and snow.

A star at the top brightly shining,
And ropes of popcorn trim,
And homemade gifts for everyone—
Joy hanging from every limb!

Stockings hung at the fireplace
To happy children's delight,
As they waited for Santa to fill them
On that long-ago Christmas night.

Candles that gleam in the windows,
And kerosene lamps that glow,
Sending their welcome greetings
Far over the drifting snow.

Even now I can hear the jingling
Of sleigh bells tinkly-bright,
Mingled with horses clomping
Through snow, on that far away night.

The holly wreath decorations,
And the mistletoe hung at the door—
Oh, bring back to me the serenity
Of an old-fashioned Christmas once more!

Angie Davidson Bass

To Our Readers,

Recently we announced plans to publish IDEALS in a smaller size with more pages. Your response was overwhelming—"Don't change!", "We love the size it is now!", "More color pictures!", and "Give us the IDEALS' beauty and quality we've treasured for 37 years!"

Therefore . . . we respect your wishes and will not change the format of IDEALS. We will keep our traditional size, but increase the number of color pages by more than 10%! We feel this will enhance your reading pleasure and add beauty to each keepsake issue!

AND . . . although we will raise the single copy price from $2.95 to $3.50, your subscription price remains unchanged for . . . BIGGER THAN EVER SAVINGS!

ONE YEAR—(8 Beautiful Issues) $15.95
a 43% SAVINGS over the single copy price.

TWO YEARS—(16 Beautiful Issues) $27.95
a 50% SAVINGS over the single copy price.

ACKNOWLEDGMENTS

OPEN THE DOOR TO CHRISTMAS by Mabel Jones Gabbott. Copyrighted. Reprinted through courtesy of *The Children's Friend*. WHERE IS THE CHRIST OF CHRISTMAS? by Marjorie Gordon. Previously published in *Aglow*. Used with permission of the author. WHAT IS CHRISTMAS? by Carol Bessent Hayman. From *What Is Christmas?* by Carol Bessent Hayman. Copyright 1974 by *Tidings*. Used by permission of Discipleship Resources, P.O. Box 840, Nashville, Tenn. 37202. Poetry by Elizabeth Searle Lamb: THE CHRISTMAS LIGHT, from *Today and Every Day*, Copyright 1970 by Unity School of Christianity, first published in *Nautilus*, Dec. 1948; CHRISTMAS MOBILE, previously published in *Capper's Weekly*; CHRISTMAS PRAYER, from *Daily Meditation* by Unity School of Christianity, Dec. 1962; CHRISTMAS SAMPLER, first published in *Capper's Weekly*; COUNT ONE, AT CHRISTMAS, first published in *Daily Meditation*, Unity School of Christianity, Nov./Dec. 1974; KALEIDOSCOPE from *Today and Every Day*, Copyright © 1970 by Unity School of Christianity; MY RESOLUTION (originally published in the Jan. 1968 issue of *Daily Word* under the title "January Resolutions"); SONG FOR DECEMBER, first published in *Capper's Weekly*; TO A FRIEND, published in *Daily Word*, Aug. 1975. All poetry used with permission of the author. GOD'S CORNER (Clasp Christmas close to you . . .) by Gertrude M. Puelicher. From *Exclusively Yours*, Dec. 2, 1977. THE GIFT by Colleen L. Reece. Previously published in *Ruralite*, Dec. 1979. CHRISTMAS EVE MOMENT by Adeline Roseberg. Previously published in *The Farmer*, Dec. 1954, St. Paul, Minn. CHRISTMAS GREETINGS and CHRISTMAS IS HAPPINESS by Helen Shick. Previously published in *The Leader-Vindicator*, New Bethlehem, Penna. A WINTER DAY by Margaret Phillips Succop in the section FOUR CHRISTMAS POEMS appeared in Mrs. Succop's volume *Climb to the Stars*, and is reprinted with permission of the copyright owner. This poem is taken from *The Christmas Book*, edited by Marion R. Todd. copyright © 1959 by Marion R. Todd, and published by The William-Frederick Press, New York, 1959. BALLAD FOR YULE by Nancy Byrd Turner. Copyrighted. Used by permission of Melvin Lee Steadman, Jr. BAYBERRIES - OUR FRAGRANT HERITAGE by Evelyn Witter. Reprinted from *Farm Wife News*, November 1974. Genesis 50:20 and Hebrews 9:11-12 in WHERE IS THE CHRIST OF CHRISTMAS? by Marjorie Gordon. Verses are taken from *The Living Bible*, copyright 1971 by Tyndale House Publishers, Wheaton, Ill. Used by permission. GINGERBREAD COOKIES recipe from *Ideals Christmas Cookbook*. Copyright © 1975 by Ideals Publishing Corporation. SPRINGERLE recipe from *Christmas Gifts From the Kitchen*, Copyright © 1976 by Ideals Publishing Corporation. Our sincere thanks to Dorothy Gladys Spicer whose address we were unable to locate for the following: MORAVIAN CHRISTMAS COOKIES, from *Feast-Day Cakes From Many Lands* by Dorothy Gladys Spicer, Copyright © 1960 by Gladys Spicer Fraser.

COLOR ART AND PHOTO CREDITS
(in order of appearance)

Front and back cover, Bob Taylor; inside front cover, Fred Sieb; Bringing in the tree, Alpha Photo Associates; Holiday cookies, Three Lions, Inc.; Winter road, Freelance Photographers Guild; A little girl's wish, Freelance Photographers Guild; THE BEAR WHO SLEPT THROUGH CHRISTMAS, Rick Reinert; Voices of Christmas, H. Armstrong Roberts; Merry Christmas morning, Alpha Photo Associates; Peeking in at Christmas, Alpha Photo Associates; A Christmas story, Tony Stone Associates; Holiday hearth, Fred Sieb; Glow of Christmas, Fred Sieb; Yuletide treats, Fred Sieb; Treasures of Christmases past, Fred Sieb; Poinsettias, Fred Sieb; Stained-glass window, Alpha Photo Associates; BIRTH OF CHRIST, Bouguereau, Three Lions, Inc.; Church interior, H. Armstrong Roberts; New England town at dusk, H. Armstrong Roberts; Outdoor splendor, Fred Sieb; Sleigh ride, H. Armstrong Roberts; Antique-furnished rooms, Mark Sexton; Old-fashioned Christmas, H. Armstrong Roberts; inside back cover, Fred Sieb.

Antiques World subscription orders, payments, inquiries, changes of address and undelivered copies should be sent to ANTIQUES WORLD Subscription Service, P.O. Box 990, Farmingdale, New York 11737. Subscription rates: $18.00 per year (Canadian/Foreign: $4.00 additional).